A TINY ACT

OF DEFIANCE

Peter J. Rivett

© 2001 Peter J. Rivett
All rights reserved. No part of this publication may be reproduced, stored in a retrieval system, or transmitted in any form or by any means, electronic, mechanical, photocopying, recording or otherwise, without the prior written permission of the publishers.

ISBN 0 953 49473 X

Published by
Planetesimal® Publishing Limited
PO Box No. 147
Paignton, Devon TQ4 6YH

Printed in England

Disclaimer of Liability

Neither Planetesimal® Publishing Limited, its employees nor anyone involved with the creation, production or distribution of this book, shall be liable for any loss or damage arising from the use or inability to use the information printed herein.

INTRODUCTION

Whilst researching for an earlier book, "Sark - A Feudal Fraud?", I came across some documents which stopped me in my tracks. This is the story of a small band of quite humble individuals, cut-off from Britain, who were determined to carry on as though war had not touched the Channel Islands. The scope of their work, their imagination, their innovation in finding ways to make quality products for the public as well as their selfless devotion to their absent employers, Boots the Chemists, really demands our respect.

Fragments of this story have been published before, mainly in professional journals and trade papers, but this is believed to be the first time that all of the pieces have been put together as a single narrative.

Peter J. Rivett
January 2001

PROLOGUE

"Perhaps it is only a tiny act of defiance to keep a chemist's shop going under German occupation. Certainly it was no more than people were doing all over the Channel Islands. Yet, if there is a single lesson that I learned from that time, it was one taught to me by the people with whom I worked. You are only defeated when you admit defeat."

Arthur F. Butterworth
Manager of Boots the Chemists
during the Occupation of Guernsey
1940-1945

CONTENTS

Chapter one
　　Prelude　　　　　　　　　　　　1

Chapter two
　　Occupation　　　　　　　　　　3

Chapter three
　　Arthur Butterworth　　　　　　7

Chapter four
　　Mathew Angell　　　　　　　　13

Chapter five
　　Public Health　　　　　　　　　19

Chapter six
　　Sadie Butterworth　　　　　　　21

Chapter seven
　　Friendly Fire !　　　　　　　　29

Chapter eight
　　Deliverance Deferred　　　　　33

Chapter nine
　　A Team Effort　　　　　　　　41

Chapter ten
　　The Captains And The Kings Depart　45

Epilogue　　　　　　　　　　　　47

Appendix 1　　　　　　　　　　48

Appendix 2　　　　　　　　　　49

Appendix 3　　　　　　　　　　50

Appendix 4　　　　　　　　　　52

The State of Play
June 1940

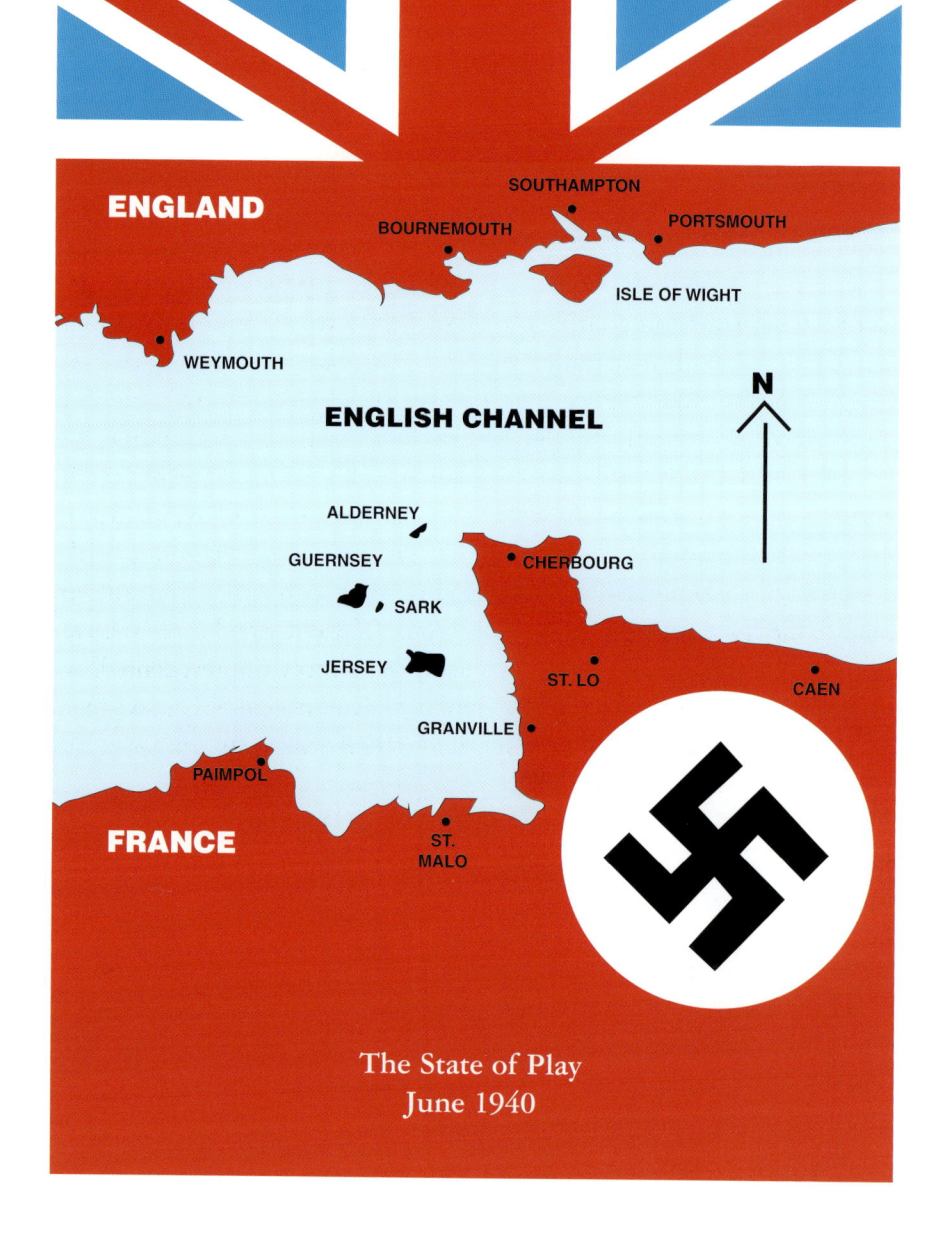

CHAPTER ONE

PRELUDE

In June 1940 the "phoney war" came to an abrupt end, with the German army sweeping all before it in their drive to conquer Western Europe. It became increasingly apparent to Channel Islanders that as the Germans moved westward the islands would be drawn into the war zone. The final signal was when Cherbourg fell and the people of Guernsey realised that if they wished to go to England, there was not a moment to lose. Very many of the inhabitants were understandably anxious and undecided. There was little official lead given and indeed, it would have been foolish to expect anyone in authority to be able to balance the "pros" of staying with the "cons" of leaving and then to issue cogent advice. An invasion of British soil was simply unprecedented, at least since the year 1066! The Procureur of Guernsey emphasised that the Bailiff, Crown Officers and Jurats of the Royal Court intended to stay at their posts. Part of an official notice read:

> "The Bailiff and the Island Administration will continue to function and it is desirable that farmers and others engaged in essential industries should stay. Please DO NOT slaughter a single animal or do anything panicky."

Placards were displayed on motor cars and hoardings with messages such as "Do Not Be Yellow" or "There Is No Place Like Home". There were chaotic scenes everywhere. Cats and dogs were put down in hundreds and when the vets ran out of cyanide, they were reduced to shooting the creatures. People were sleeping in the open awaiting their turn to embark. Cattle were left roaming about by departed owners and cars and property were given away to friends, by word of mouth. These latter transactions were later declared to be unlawful.

British forces were withdrawn from the Channel Islands and those civilians who desired to leave were evacuated in three liners and the regular mail boats which ran to the very last. Many boatloads of refugees from France had arrived, these were fed, provided with clothing and sent off to the British mainland. Some 17,000 out of a pre-war population of 42,000 decided to leave. Panic set in after the military and children had left and there were long queues at the banks to withdraw savings, indeed it was almost impossible to get near the banks at any time of the day. Once the last boat had sailed, the islanders sat back to await their fate.

CHAPTER TWO

OCCUPATION

On 30th June 1940 Guernsey was invaded. In spite of the German Army and Navy having complex plans for a frontal assault, code named "Operation Grüne Pfeile", it was the Luftwaffe who effectively seized the island. Several reconnaissance flights were made in the days leading up to 30th June and on 28th June German planes bombed the harbour at St Peter Port, killing thirty-two persons and injuring thirty-three. They claimed to have been misled into thinking that a long queue of tomato lorries was, in fact, an army convoy. An ambulance was strafed out in the country and the driver killed, over 150 bullet holes were counted in the vehicle. Even the lifeboat en route to Jersey was attacked, with one fatality and the mail steamer "Courier" returning from Alderney was repeatedly fired upon but due to the skill of the captain, the vessel was unscathed.

The Germans then landed at the island airport and took control of Guernsey. Thus was completed a run of successes for the Nazis which started with Poland and ended at the British dependent territories of the Channel Islands. "Next stop England" proclaimed the Germans.

As it turned out, they were wrong and thus the Channel Islands were the only places where the German administrative machine ran up against the British psyche. Without doubt, the occupying forces had been given orders to be "nice guys". No raping nuns or waving babies on the end of bayonets as was rumoured to have happened elsewhere.

By being reasonably considerate, it was hoped that word would get through to the "appeasers" in London that the Nazis were not such bad chaps after all. However, it was always going to be the iron fist in the velvet glove. The official occupation of Guernsey commenced on Monday 1st July 1940 and residents going to work were met with the distinctly un-British sight of armed guards on telephone exchanges, cross-roads and at the Post Office. Clocks were advanced one hour to German Summer Time.

At first the German soldiers were thrilled by the abundance of consumer goods on display in the local shops and by means of a favourable exchange rate, were able to soon strip the shelves bare of cameras, films, perfumes, toiletries, cloth, etc. which were swiftly sent back home to Germany. It was the boast of German officers that "we will have the cloth suitings made up in Saville Row in September". With a rate of exchange initially heavily weighted in favour of the occupying forces, these items were dirt cheap. On 2nd July 1940, the German Mark was provisionally fixed at five to the Pound. It then fluctuated until 21st August 1941 when it was pegged at 9.36 Marks to the Pound. This last rate was described as ridiculous because half-pennies were lost in the exchange.

Copper coins became virtually non-existent because they, like their higher-value silver counterparts, were soon taken out of circulation by the occupiers seeking souvenirs to send home. Occasionally one might see 5 pfg and 10 pfg coins but in general, the giving of change was a problem for all Guernsey shops. In April 1941, the States of Guernsey issued paper notes in denominations of 6d, 1/3d, 2/6d and 5/- to try to alleviate the shortage of silver coins, but for some reason these were described as totally inadequate and became quite rare.

Initially there was an abundance of consumer goods. Being an island, the wholesalers and retailers of Guernsey kept higher stock levels than their mainland counterparts. In the brief period when the civilian population was reduced by evacuation and the German garrison had not yet been built up to the extremely high levels eventually achieved, there were few shortages. This situation was, however, short-lived. As items sold out, little was available to replace them, for the Channel Islands imported most of their manufactured goods from the UK and this route was, of course, closed. Soon the shops were looking very spartan which though mildly inconvenient for the occupying forces, was to become a critical problem for the islanders. Not until stocks had reached a very low level was any attempt made to ration the military although the civilian population was rationed from the outset. Not only were food and other consumer goods rationed, but supplies of electricity, gas and other fuels were strictly curtailed.

The years of occupation were to be humdrum. There was little by way of relaxation and even less of excitement. Occasionally, the Royal Air Force bombed the harbour or the airport. During the Battle of Britain, the sky over Guernsey was used as a rendezvous for German aircraft to get into formation prior to setting off for Britain and islanders had the sad sight of bombers en route to bomb English towns. This was doubly sad because so many islanders had been evacuated to towns on the south coast of England.

Such imported supplies as there were arrived via the French port of Granville, whilst St Malo supplied the German garrison. Gradually, the Germans built up the defences and it seemed obvious that the intention was to turn Guernsey into a fortress. To achieve this they imported thousands of foreign labourers who were given just sufficient food to enable them to work. It was a sad sight to see these men lined up, in rags and clearly ill, with their tin mugs for a ration of soup. Diseases such as typhus and scabies were prevalent amongst these people. Tunnels were dug underground and great gun emplacements constructed, most of which remain to this day as a testament of man's inhumanity to his fellow man.

As the population swelled by the importation of military and forced labour, so, because of German interference, the productivity of the land declined. There were often no potatoes, only swedes, parsnips and carrots, and these in very limited quantities. The ration of cooking fat was dispensed with and meat was strictly rationed at first to 6 ounces per head per week and then to 4 ounces per head per month. Milk had been separated from the start of the Occupation with the cream going to the German officers. Indeed, it is rumoured that in the first few months of occupation, it was not unknown for jackboots to be cleaned with best Guernsey butter although this is probably apocryphal.

Occasionally, there was fish to be had in the shops, but only what was left after the Germans had taken the best. The early shopping sprees had denuded the island of footwear. A supply of poor quality shoes with wooden soles was obtained from France but these commanded a very high price. The States Purchasing Commission was often reduced to buying goods from the French "Black Market" but these goods were both expensive and of an inferior quality. Dress material normally retailing at 4/11d (25p) per yard, cost £2 per yard. Mens' underwear was £3 per set. Ladies stockings, when obtainable, cost 25/- (£1.25) against a pre-war price of 2/11d (15p).

A Black Market appeared on Guernsey. Butter ranged from 10/- to 50/- per lb (50p to £2.50) until 1944 when it became unobtainable. Meat, when it could be found, was 22/6d per lb (£1.12p). Rabbits were 55/- each (£2.75p), Eggs 2/1d (10p) each. English tobacco, a very rare commodity, commanded the staggering price of £112 per lb. A baby's teat fetched £3/10/0d (£3.50p) and tea was £20 per lb, if one could get it!

One shining beacon amongst all of this racketeering was the local branch of Boots the Chemists which was generally accepted to be the only shop in Guernsey which managed to maintain its pre-war appearance, prices and quality. Why this was so will be shown in succeeding chapters.

CHAPTER THREE

ARTHUR BUTTERWORTH

Boots the Chemists, that old established concern whose unofficial motto was "We supply everything except the baby" was, and indeed still is, located in the High Street of St Peter Port. In those days, their premises were much like the chemists now seen in "heritage centres", with the windows filled with large glass bottles of coloured liquid and, behind the counter, dark wooden drawers labelled with incomprehensible chemical names and abbreviations.

They were to run short of proprietary items much sooner than the independent chemists because whereas the latter had to stock up well in advance of sales, Boots on the other hand, always had a mainland depot to call upon for replacements to their inventory and thus had no need to over-stock.

There is a very strong link between Boots and the Channel Islands, indeed the link is so strong that it is sometimes said that Boots the Chemists was founded in Jersey but that honour lies firmly with Nottingham. In 1886, Jesse Boot owner of a small chain of pharmacies in Nottingham was recuperating in Jersey from overwork and stress. He had tried to sell his business without much success and when his health suffered, he travelled to Jersey. There he met Florence Rowe, the daughter of a local bookseller and stationer who traded in St Helier. In August 1886, they were married, he was 36, she 23. Florence, having learned much from her father about business methods became closely involved with her husband's undertaking. She was especially interested in developing Boots Booklovers Libraries and the Boots cafés. Florence must have been a very emancipated lady, for in addition to her business interests, she took on responsibility for staff welfare and developed what was to become a "family aura" about working for Boots the Chemists. In 1896, ten years after the marriage, Boots opened premises in Queen Street, St Helier. Later a branch was opened in St Peter Port, Guernsey.

The Manager of the Guernsey branch in 1940 was an Englishman, Arthur Butterworth. He qualified as a pharmacist shortly after the Great War, having served as a wireless operator in the Merchant Navy and having had three ships torpedoed beneath him. It is difficult to imagine the predicament in which he now found himself. One day, he was manager of a small branch of a very large company with all of the support he needed to run the business and the next day he was very much his own man. Was he still an employee, or were "all bets off" once the Germans moved in?

No-one would have blamed him if he had just locked up the shop and walked away. After all, he was not one of the owners of Boots, merely a paid employee and neither was he a native of Guernsey. Why should he go out on a limb to look after property which belonged to shareholders in England who might find themselves in the same boat in the very near future? In fact, he was expected, by his Territorial General Manager to close the shop and leave the island with everyone else. Arthur Butterworth was, however, adamant. "My duty is with my staff and shop and to the people of Guernsey - we shall stay."

It reflects greatly to his credit that he and his staff carried on working and made every effort to conduct "business as normal". It reflects also great credit on Boots the Chemists Ltd for inculcating such loyalty in their staff. Today, when the term "duty" merely refers to an amount of tax which can be avoided by illicitly bringing in consumer goods from overseas, this story is a fine example of persons not letting the mere occupation of their homeland by a foreign army prevent them from doing that which they considered to be their duty.

At first it was business as normal. The German Authorities had decreed that things were to go on as before. True, the staff had some difficulty in understanding what the new customers wanted and instead of Pound notes, they had to take Occupation Reichmarks over the counter but business was brisk. Later, their role took a much more serious turn when the supply of medicines dried up and innovation became the order of the day.

Actually, the artificial shopping spree had started, as far as Boots was concerned, in the last week of June as people were hurriedly buying stocks to take away with them. Many islanders had never travelled far and their first requirement was for suitcases and trunks. Indeed, the shop sold out completely of these items. One morning, they had over 1,000 customers and took £270 in a very short time. Because change was unobtainable, a "counter bill" was supplied to the customer, in lieu of change, which could be cashed in at any branch of Boots on the mainland. Quite why persons who knew they were leaving for England should want to denude the shops of items which those left behind might well be desperate for, is unclear. The first month of occupation turned in normal levels of takings, an average of £650 per week. This average declined to £326 by the end of 1940.

The first test of Mr. Butterworth's initiative came when it was realised that tomatoes, the traditional cash crop of Guernsey, had yielded a bumper harvest in 1940 which in normal times would have been good news were it not for the fact that there was no longer an export market. The surplus ran to thousands of tons and the States of Guernsey realised that they had to act quickly and find a way of preserving some of the crop for use at a future date. One of the methods used was to pickle the tomatoes in huge brine tanks and Mr. Butterworth was asked to conduct a feasibility study. It seemed to be a simple enough task at first, all one had to do was to convert sea water into brine. However, upon being informed that no power or solid fuel could be used, that idea was quickly cast aside.

After much thought, Arthur Butterworth designed an apparatus which first saw the light of day in Saxon times. Under the shadow of Castle Cornet, there is a splendid boating pond where generations of Guernsey children, not to mention Guernsey adults have sailed yachts and other model boats. He constructed a structure of scaffold poles, etc., about 60 feet long and 20 feet high the whole to be placed over the concrete pond. The structure was then filled with brushwood and with the aid of a crude windmill, seawater was pumped up to a trough running the length of the structure. This permitted the water to percolate through the brushwood back into the pond. The wind blowing through the brushwood caused some of the water content to evaporate to the extent that by the time the water had reached the concrete tank, its salinity had been slightly enhanced. This was repeated over and over again, until the brine was of the required strength. There was an amusing side-effect to this operation. Somehow, sloe bushes were mixed amongst the brushwood and this coloured the brine a sort of "pinky-mauve". Housewives reported that it looked a little odd, but otherwise, was quite acceptable. Later on, much to his relief, some steam power was made available and still using Mr. Butterworth's crude plant, brine and dry salt were recovered from seawater.

As well as this ancient method, Mrs. Butterworth gave demonstrations on how to preserve tomatoes using the considerably more modern Kilner jars. Mrs. Butterworth had completed some of the work towards becoming a chemist but upon marriage gave it up to run the home which was commonplace in those days. However, as will be seen, Mrs. Butterworth was to make a very significant contribution to the success of Boots in those dark years.

Soon after the Occupation, the island's chemists held a meeting to discuss the possibility of obtaining supplies from Occupied Europe. On behalf of Boots, Mr. Butterworth agreed that his shop would undertake the warehousing and distribution of goods and that he would share out the products at cost plus 2.5% to cover porterage etc. This did not, in the event, cover the extra costs and Mr. Butterworth subsequently learnt that his opposite number in Jersey, Mr. Gould was getting a 7.5% mark-up.

The first order was sent off by Mr. R Falla, the States "Buyer" who contacted the firm of Jean Langlois in Rennes and this proved a useful source for subsequent supplies. Many of the fine chemicals were supplied by Rhone Poulenc of Paris and these were of excellent quality. However, other drugs supplied by Jean Langlois were often very badly packed in 20kg or 30kg paper bags and consequently attracted a very high wastage rate. Any drugs which raised doubts as to their pureness were sent to the States of Guernsey's analyst, Mr. Allerton, who in the course of the Occupation carried out several hundred such analyses.

In August 1940, Mr. Butterworth had a stroke of luck. The Gestapo visited the shop to examine the contents of the library. Before the war and indeed, for many years afterwards, Boots maintained a first class lending library, sadly, now no more. The Gestapo removed a number of books which they felt were anti-German, including some Penguin books which carried cartoons of Hitler and his gang drawn by the celebrated caricaturist, David Low.

The interpreter who accompanied the Gestapo officer mentioned in passing that before the war he had been employed by a firm who dealt in ethical drugs and he was asked by Mr. Butterworth if he could put Boots in contact with them. Since the interpreter seemed agreeable, Mr. Butterworth gave him a list of Bayer's products which were urgently needed by the hospitals and for dispensing. He was later informed that the interpreter's firm, Messrs A Krause & Co. of Kleine Reichenstrasse, Hamburg had booked the order and all that was needed to trigger delivery was the little matter of payment in advance.

All that Mr. Butterworth had in the till were Occupation Marks which were not valid within Germany but the interpreter suggested that he could send a corporal home on leave with the cash, which he would convert in Holland to "real" Marks and hand it on to Krause and Co. This put Mr. Butterworth on the spot. The cost was RM 4000, or about £400 and he was having to give it to an enemy chap he hardly knew who was giving it to another enemy chap, who, it was hoped, would pass it on to an enemy supplier. It had all the hallmarks of a "con" but Arthur Butterworth decided to chance it and was rewarded in due course, with a very useful consignment of drugs.

Arthur Butterworth spoke extremely highly of Krause and Co. who packed all consignments very well and honoured, to the letter, any claims for shortages or breakages. He was full of praise for the fairness of treatment and the goods supplied were of inestimable value to the entire community. As well as "fine" chemicals from Schering, Merck and other well known German firms, he was able to acquire saccharin tablets, teats, razor blades, Sanatogen, adhesive plaster, cotton-wool, serums, insulin, syringes, dental plaster, toothbrushes and disinfecting fluid. One item greatly needed which Krause & Co. were able to supply were 100,000 waxed ointment boxes from Czechoslovakia. These were invaluable, for without them Boots would not have been able to retail their various product lines.

As food supplies diminished diets became very unbalanced, and thus the incidence of illness increased. Arthur Butterworth realised that the demand for medical products would also increase and unless someone was prepared to have a go at manufacturing them, a lack of medication would compound the other privations the islanders had to suffer. The premises at Boots were neither equipped nor intended for manufacturing but the photographic developing room, ladies tea room and a downstairs cellar were adapted for this purpose. Arthur Butterworth and his pharmacist, Matthew Angell started work and some of their early output included Phos Tonic, Influenza mixture, embrocation, indigestion mixtures and bronchial lozenges. A full list of drugs manufactured or prepared is shown in Appendix 1.

CHAPTER FOUR

MATTHEW ANGELL

The second man at Boots, Matthew Angell, was born in Alderney in 1913. He started work at Boots in 1930 after leaving Elizabeth College and spent four years as an apprentice starting on a wage of 10/0d (50p) a week. He then went to Portsmouth Municipal College and qualified as a pharmacist. As soon as his name was inscribed on the rolls of the Pharmaceutical Society of Great Britain, his wage reached £4 a week, a good wage in those days. When the Occupation commenced, he was drug manager at Boots in the High Street, St Peter Port. His wife was, from 1940, a complete invalid and gravely ill until she died in August 1942.

There is a saying that "no-one is indispensable". Matthew Angell came as near to disproving that saying as is ever likely to happen. He gave unstinted service to the firm, putting in much extra time, Sundays, half days (when shops closed) and evenings. He had a hand in almost every innovation or experiment and was a powerhouse of new ideas. As if this was not enough, he lectured in Pharmacy and Dispensing for new members of staff, doctors' dispensers and anyone else who showed an interest in pharmacy. These lectures were held in conjunction with chemistry classes held by the States Analyst and as there was no adult education in Guernsey, they proved to be a great boon. In his spare time (!), he proved useful in an advisory capacity to the Health Services Officer, local doctors and the States Analyst as well as being an expert witness on milk analysis in the Royal Court of Guernsey. Matthew Angell went without a holiday for five years. The only time he was absent was when, after the death of his wife, he failed to take care of himself and thus was struck down with pleurisy which resulted in his absence from work for two weeks.

Realising very early on in the Occupation that proprietary medicines might be in short supply, Matthew Angell started to consider manufacturing "galenicals". These were medicinal compounds using natural substances and were named after one of the "greats" in pharmaceuticals, Galen (130-200 AD). Thus tomato growers were persuaded to set land aside to grow belladonna, capsicum, digitalis and opium poppies from seeds purchased in France, for use by Matthew, in his professional capacity of course! The island was searched for anything which might be useful. A closed lemonade factory produced saccharin. Beekeepers were prevailed upon to part with their beeswax. A disused soap works produced barrels of fat, useful after sterilisation, for the manufacture of ointments. Iodine used to be manufactured from seaweed on the island of Lihou in the 1920's and a large jar of iodine crystals, previously overlooked, was swiftly gathered into the Boots net. Volk, a red spider spray was found to be useful in the manufacture of hair cream. Oddest of all, a local chap arrived with four large sacks of corks which he had hoarded since a shipwreck in 1902. A further bonus turned up when a Mr. Luxon, who suffered from asthma, asked the German harbourmaster if there was any possibility that he could obtain supplies of Ephedrine tablets which were needed to combat the ailment. The harbourmaster, who was going on leave to France brought back with him 10,000 tablets, far more than Mr. Luxon might need in a lifetime. These were offered to Boots on condition that there would always be a supply for Mr. Luxon when he needed them. Mr. Angell swiftly agreed and took the tablets into stock.

Throughout the Occupation, Matthew Angell was proud of the fact that his dispensing must, and did, adhere to Boots high standards. Despite paper shortages, enough was acquired to send out all bottles neatly wrapped. Bottles of medicines were, in those days, sealed with red sealing wax, and this practice was continued during the war.

Tablets were packed in small envelopes and wedding cake boxes were used for other items. Prescriptions filled averaged about 500 per month.

With the unusual ingredients at his disposal, together with a food mixer obtained from a nearby cake shop, and a copy of the Encyclopaedia Britannica (1890 edition!) Matthew Angell commenced work. Prior to the outbreak of war, pharmaceuticals were made to the BP standard and this was shown on the bottle or packet. Matthew Angell decided to use the letters EF, standing for "emergency formula" for it was often impossible to adhere strictly to the BP standards. As well as the cake mixer, a coffee grinder was pressed into service. Lozenges were cut to shape with an apple corer and extracts obtained with a meat press acquired from a butcher. A tincture of capsicum pepper was mixed with grease to make a quite acceptable substitute for Thermogene Rub.

One of the "treats" meted out to children in pre-war Britain was cod liver oil. Likewise in Guernsey. Mothers regarded this as a sort of essential elixir. Most children regarded it with absolute dread! If they were lucky, all they had to do was to swallow a capsule but the majority of children had to take it by spoonful once a day. Once tasted, never forgotten.

Cod liver oil is an important source of vitamins A and D. It assists teeth, bone and skin growth. A lack of these vitamins reduces the eyesight and then produces dry skin, itchy eyes, rashes and a general susceptibility to infection. In Guernsey it was obtained from the UK, the main brands being "Boots", "Seven Seas" and "Crookes". Matthew Angell was concerned that before stocks ran out, a substitute had to be found. The question was, from where? By chance, he just happened to have a learned treatise on experiments made in Germany in the use of fish oils written by a Guernseyman, Dr. Edward Carey, long before vitamins were ever thought of. The irony of this connection, Guernsey with Germany would not have been lost on Matthew.

Although livers from the cod fish seem to have been used by the "trade" to the effect that cod liver oil had almost become a generic name, the fact is that the cod's liver is by no means the most nutritious, the oil from a halibut's liver being considerably higher in nutritional value. Matthew Angell decided to see if livers from other fish would do equally as well as a substitute and accordingly conducted a number of experiments.

The sawmills at La Piette had been made available to the States of Guernsey and it was decided to use the laboratory there to prepare livers for conversion to oil. Using a dairy pan lent by the manager of the States dairy, the well-washed livers were stewed until a crude oil was produced and this was drawn off to the storage tanks. The livers then went through a secondary process at a higher temperature to obtain further oils which were not so prolific in vitamins.

Not content with two processes, the mass of livers were then subjected to a mechanical press, much like a cider press, where the last drop of oil was squeezed out. The three grades of oil were then subjected to various purification processes. The next question was, "is this oil any good?" To find out, he advertised in the local press for mice (any colour) but the response was so poor that he had to settle for the humble guinea pig. He then carried out a series of chemically and biologically controlled experiments (Appendix 3) and concluded "This oil has ample amounts of Vitamins A and D ". Fishermen were urged to save all fish livers for use by Mr. Angell and his colleagues. Thus were the children of Guernsey assured of a continuing supply of "cod" liver oil and although they never knew it, they had cause to be very thankful that Matthew had taken the trouble to investigate how to overcome what otherwise would have been a serious deficiency.

German troops were not allowed to purchase medicines in local chemists. It is thought that the reason for this rule was to prevent them trying to treat themselves for ailments which more properly ought to have been dealt with by the Unit Medical Officer. Matthew recalls that one Saturday, he was warned by the Germans to present himself the following Sunday morning to attend an investigation into a prescription containing codeine which he had filled for a German soldier. He remembers that it was a very cold day, and wrapped up in as many coats as he could muster, he was ushered into an ante room wherein was a fire of such magnificent proportions as to nearly bring tears to his eyes. He had neither seen such a fire, nor felt such warmth in years. The investigation was conducted mainly in German, with such questions as were put in English seemingly taking him to be a Doctor. The problem arose because the UK and the Channel Islands used apothecaries weights and measures whereas on the Continent, they used the metric system. Since every pharmacist had learned by rote that 1 gram = 15.432 grains he tried in vain to get this message across to the Germans who obviously believed that Matthew had over-prescribed by a factor of fifteen! Matthew understood little of what was going on, and in due course was ushered out. The local police chief later told him that it was believed that the soldier was trying to "work his ticket". German customers, incidentally, had to be given priority and be served before anyone else upon pain of dire punishment.

On 8th February 1945, Mathew and Daphne Angel were married. Their wedding presents included, amongst other things, a tin of salmon, soap, a pound of sugar, half a pint of paraffin, a bottle of furniture polish and a tree for firewood. These gifts may, in the 21st century, sound bizarre, but in 1945 in occupied Guernsey, they were more welcome than a dozen pop-up toasters or fondue sets! Even weddings did not escape the emergency regulations. The happy couple had to keep their fingers crossed that no-one died immediately before the ceremony because funerals took priority over weddings for use of the horse and carriage which took them to church.

CHAPTER FIVE

PUBLIC HEALTH

It is a truism that the health of a western orientated population can, within reason, improve with a little less food. This is generally preached by persons who have been spared that experience! Nevertheless, it is a fact that there were certain benefits which accrued to the public health position of islanders as a result of food rationing. This was likewise true in wartime England, indeed, it has been said that the health of the British population went downhill once rationing was removed. What is of vital importance however, is that the reduction in calorie intake should be of a balanced nature. Once the diet gets out of balance, unpleasant effects start to be felt.

By virtue of escapees and smuggled reports, the Home Office in London had a fairly accurate picture of the food situation in Guernsey and estimated that the average intake provided something between 2,000 and 2,500 calories per head per day. After D-Day and especially when German forces were expelled from the Cotentin Peninsula, the daily intake plummeted rapidly to near starvation levels.

An early manifestation of the unbalanced diet was a universal loosening of the bowels. This was ascribed to the coarseness of the new diet which in contrast to peacetime diets was deficient in roughage and caused what was known in Jersey as the "Jersey Rattles" and in Guernsey as the "Guernsey Gallop".

Weight loss was commonplace and for some, it provided new found energy. One Guernsey man dropped from a pre-war 18 stones to 8 stones, and felt all the better for it. Many women who had given up hope of bearing children suddenly found themselves pregnant and this was linked to weight loss around the abdominal area and the additional exercise brought about by removal of private and public transport coupled, no doubt, with the new-found energy of the slimmer Guernsey man!

The incidence of appendicitis, colds and peptic ulcers fell dramatically. Cardiac failures decreased also. On the other side of the coin, German soldiers sent to Guernsey for "Rest and Recreation" brought a number of diseases relatively unknown to the island, such as infective gingivitis and venereal disease. Typhus broke out but seemed to pass the civilian population by. Diabetics were the hardest hit because there was a marked lack of insulin and serious sufferers were generally hospitalised and few, if any, survived the war. It was thought that a lot of the insulin sent by the Red Cross had been intercepted and stolen in France where it fetched high prices on the "Black Market".

Notwithstanding the privations and the poor and unbalanced diet, the general health of the islanders was good. Children scored very highly in the dental stakes because they were denied chocolate, sugar and other tooth decaying products. However, they were also judged to be somewhat below size for their ages. Without the likes of Arthur Butterworth and Matthew Angell and their counterparts throughout the islands however, matters might well have been much worse.

CHAPTER SIX

SADIE BUTTERWORTH

Mrs. Sadie Butterworth, the wife of Arthur Butterworth, had been an assistant in a chemist's shop in the UK and it is believed that this is how she met her husband. Thus, although not formally qualified, she would undoubtedly have gained a smattering of technical skill. Upon marriage, as was the convention in those days, she left her employment to keep the home fires burning. However, there being little by way of home fires to keep burning during the Occupation, she volunteered to help out at her husband's workplace.

She took charge of the Toiletry Department which was fast running out of items to sell, there being no replacements from England. She therefore formed "The Toiletry Manufacturing Department" with the aim of making substitute toilet preparations. The first few months was spent in foraging. Anything not required in the other departments was swiftly purloined. Raw materials, such as bottles, jars and tins from a sweet manufacturer, all kinds of packing paper, gilt string, cords, ribbons, practically all of the Turkish towelling available in Guernsey, bindings, cottons, silks, and oils and greases from garages were purchased from sources around the island. Mrs. Butterworth calculated that the occupation would last until 1942.

The new department was soon churning out manufactured goods such as brilliantine, hair cream (oily and non-oily) talcum powder, baby powder, wave-setting lotion, lemon hand-cream and hair tonic. Bath salts, in lavender, cologne and verbena, were packed in tins for the Christmas season. Smelling salts, washing squares and gloves were also produced.

Bottles and pots were only obtained by customers returning them, or perhaps, from salvage. Ice cream cartons were brought into use for packaging talcum powder, tooth powder and baby powder. 24th December 1940 saw a consignment of goods from France including such useful raw materials as talcum, calcium carbonate and magnesium carbonate.

These products might seem at first glance to be almost a waste of resources, but the effect on civilian morale of being able to buy some of the little luxuries of life cannot be over-stated. During the first part of 1941, output increased to the extent that another junior assistant had to be engaged. Supplies were always erratic but ingenuity, more often than not, found a way around the shortages. Hair cream became a problem as supplies of tragacanth powder ran out but Mrs. Butterworth soon came up with a substitute using linseed suitably coloured and perfumed. When the linseed ran out, she evolved another but more ingenious solution.

A type of seaweed known as carrageen moss grows around the coasts of the Channel Islands. There was already a small supply in the drug department so Mrs. Butterworth experimented and discovered that suitably treated, it made quite an acceptable hair cream. She took two of the girl assistants from Boots and went off to the beaches to find the moss. Fortunately, the beaches were not mined at that date, so bathing costumes were donned and into the sea they went. There were several types of moss but the best grew on the west coast of Guernsey. Picking had to be swift, since the best quality moss grew "at the bottom of the tide". Some 3 cwt was recovered and carried back to the shop by the porters employed by Boots. (Later Boots contracted with local fishermen to collect the moss.)

The next day the moss had to be washed many times to remove the salt and other impurities and then laid out in the sun to dry and bleach. It was a long arduous job but eventually, they had enough moss to make sufficient hair cream to last for a year. The attributes of carrageen soon spread and a craze developed to the extent that it was on sale in many shops, including the Singer Sewing Machine shop. It was used in fruit jellies, blancmanges and, since Mrs. Butterworth was able to "acquire" five gallons of glycerine, in hand-care lotion as well.

Nothing succeeds like success and Sadie, triumphant from the carageen episode, made further increases in her range of home-produced toiletries. "Deodor", for excessive perspiration, Rose Hand-Cream, Buttermilk Lotion, Camphor and Quinine Hair Tonic, which one assumes had the dual utility of keeping both the moth and the mosquito away! Toothpaste, After-shave Lotion, Foot Powder, Shaving Cream, Cuticle Remover and Face Powder, (in rachel, peach and natural shades no less!) were all added to the shelves. The toothpaste, which was made in an electric food mixer, contained glycerine and carrageen emulsion and achieved record sales.

In 1941, a wholesale operation was commenced, with Boots supplying seven island hairdressers with hair cream, wave setting lotion, brilliantine cream and special solutions for those "perms" so essential to the ladies in the 1940's. Hospitals were also supplied with large quantities of dusting powder. For Christmas of that year, Mrs. Butterworth went all out for a big morale boosting show centred around coloured and perfumed bath crystals packed in attractive jars, cellophane-wrapped and beribboned. Also offered to a disbelieving public were sachets of Sark lavender supplied by Miss Ethel Cheesewright, the well-known Sark artist.

The enterprise almost came to a grinding halt on 17th September 1942 when, in common with many other British-born islanders, Mr. & Mrs. Butterworth received their marching orders for internment in Germany. Fortunately, officials of the States of Guernsey were able to convince the German High Command that Mr. & Mrs. Butterworth filled a vital role in the machinery of public health and the internment notice was rescinded. Another local chemist was not so lucky. Messrs Dupuys was then owned by a Miss Dupuy who employed a qualified manager to run the establishment; he was deported. It was decreed that all poisons would be removed from Dupuy's shop and Mr. & Mrs. Butterworth together with Matthew Angell were to take an inventory.

During the stock-take, Sadie Butterworth delved into the cellar and found old and forgotten perfume oils, fixatives and blenders, also boxes of grimy perfume bottles of elegant shapes and clearly of French manufacture. In addition, there were cut-glass smelling salt bottles together with an assortment of more recent synthetic perfumes all of which Mrs. Butterworth acquired on behalf of Messrs Boots.

Although Messrs Dupuys had imported synthetic extracts from England with which to blend perfumes, a bottle was found dated 1885 which could be truly described as vintage and certainly was "the real stuff". Since the contents of this bottle pre-dated synthetic aromatics, it had, like a fine wine, improved with age. Mrs. Butterworth wrote that this discovery gave her a thrill on a par with that of the successful archaeologist as she had often thought about making perfume but lacked the necessary oils and fixatives.

By reading back numbers of the "Pharmaceutical Journal" and the "Chemist and Druggist" Mrs. Butterworth was able to experiment until, in time for Christmas week 1942, she was able to offer to the public a choice of first class perfumes with such evocative titles as Les Fleurs, Violet, Gardenia, Orchid, Carnation, Lilac, Muguet and Imperial Chypre, as well as Cologne and Lavender Water. All of these exciting products were packed in the now sparkling clean elegant French perfume bottles. The perfume counter at Boots that year was well up to Bond Street standards as was evidenced by the takings, £322 for the Christmas period alone. The effect on Guernsey ladies must have been simply electric! In a complete reversal of roles, Boots then obtained a contract to supply Messrs Dupuys with perfume and toiletry lines which lasted until June 1943.

In 1943, the production line was kept at full throttle. Face powder was discontinued because adequate supplies from the House of Houbigant were available. However, no-one thought to supply powder puffs so once again, Mrs. Butterworth stepped into the breech. She designed a powder puff made from velour hot-water bottle covers. Since there were no hot water bottles to be had, keeping the covers seemed pointless so why not utilise them in other ways? These were cut to shape, stuffed with sterile kapok and finished with a cord loop. Packed in a cellophane envelope, these proved to be an instant success.

Home grown tobacco had long been a bit of a trial to smoke. Indeed, a local joke was that the "scorched earth" policy originated in the tobacco fields of Guernsey! In the summer of 1943, Sadie Butterworth invented a new perfume, "Fleur de Tabac" and soon the word got around the island that this was just what was needed to make smoking a local cigarette bearable. From then until September, when the local tobacco crop was finished, Boots was besieged by the most unlikely male customers seeking to buy perfume!

Christmas 1943 saw an even greater demand for Boots home produced perfumes. Although the shop now had a supply of French perfumes, these were mostly of the heavy ("tarty") type not appealing to the more genteel taste of the Guernsey lady. Mrs. Butterworth set her "own brand" perfumes a sales target of £600 for Christmas week and in fact took £621.

1944 opened on an optimistic and expectant note but everything changed on 6th June 1944, D-Day. When it became clear that liberation of the Channel Islands was not, nor could be, a high priority, life for the population of Guernsey turned very nasty.

When Normandy fell, Boots received a bit of a windfall, the usefulness of which was clouded by the deteriorating food situation. The Germans shut the military brothels and returned the girls to the mainland. A truckload of luxury toiletries became available and was delivered to Boots. It was later discovered that these "ladies of the night" had been granted rations equivalent to heavy workers for the heroic part they played in support of the German war effort!

Mrs. Butterworth noted that in anticipation of the lack of fuel supplies, she had manufactured sufficient hair cream and tooth powder to last until the end of February 1945 by which time "if the island is not relieved, we shall be without bread and other essential foodstuffs and it will take all our energies to survive". Mrs Sadie Butterworth recorded a few statistics.

From mid 1942 until October 1944, when production dried up, the number of bottles washed and packed averaged five hundred per week. Some four hundred cartons of all shapes and sizes were packed every week. Eight hundred gallons of brilliantine hair-cream had been manufactured.

The prices charged were commensurate with the cost of materials and, as far as possible, were kept to pre-war levels. A full list of goods manufactured is shown in Appendix 2.

Mrs. Butterworth was something of a visionary. In 1940 she thought the occupation would last two years, whereas the Germans thought it would all be over by Christmas 1940. She produced certain goods in advance based upon liberation taking place in Feb 1945, it turned out to be May 1945. However, what is more impressive is that in 1942 and 1943 she quietly obtained red, white and blue bunting and crepe paper to be made up into Victory favours in 1944.

Mrs. Butterworth was mindful that what she achieved was not by her efforts alone and she paid fulsome tributes to Miss Gorelle and Miss Gilman, her "factory hands" as well as Mrs. Rich and the girls who made up the counter and window displays. She wrote "*They have worked so well and so cheerfully to help me maintain the high quality and cleanliness expected of Boots products*". The fact that underlying her work throughout the Occupation was the desire to maintain the quality of Boots reputation betokens loyalty of a very high order. She was not even officially an employee although she was later paid for the hours she had worked.

Little of what Mrs. Butterworth manufactured could have been claimed to have been absolutely essential. However, the effect upon the morale of the inhabitants of Guernsey must have been very profound. What the effect must have been on the German administration who witnessed one single shop produce luxury item after luxury item with no obvious source of supply, will never be known. It might well have been an object lesson as to why they were losing the war!

CHAPTER SEVEN

FRIENDLY FIRE !

At around midnight on 14th August 1944, British warships shelled the harbour of St Peter Port and a number of projectiles landed within the confines of the town. At 2.00 a.m. Sergeant Bob Kimber of the Guernsey Constabulary received a call from the Germans requesting a police presence at Messrs Boots in the High Street. Constables Peadon and Le Poidevin attended the scene and found water pouring out of the premises of Boots, and Messrs Hipps, into the Crown Hotel and Messrs Delas, the ladies outfitters. A search for the stopcock to the water main proved fruitless so the water board were summoned. The Germans insisted that Arthur Butterworth be roused to open the shop so that the damage could be assessed. At about 3.00 a.m. Arthur Butterworth was collected from his home in King's Road and in darkness, duly entered and inspected the premises.

A 4.7" shell had severed the main pipe which supplied the sprinkler system. Arthur Butterworth found the ceilings dripping with water, not unlike a sharp rain shower and six inches of water had accumulated in the cellars. The shell, which weighed about 28lbs, had burst the pipe which in turn deflected it through the floor into the lending library. There it hit a main girder which further deflected it onto the wall. After hitting the wall, it came to rest on the floor of the library. Thankfully, it did not explode. Arthur Butterworth had hoped to keep the shell as a souvenir but the following morning a German bomb disposal team called to take it away.

Most of the books in the library were saturated and over 200 volumes were beyond repair and were rendered useless. The electrics of Boots and adjoining premises had all fused and were irreparable. As a result, the department had to be closed for three days. Damp books were taken up to the attic to dry out. Fortunately it was summer and the library staff worked hard for three days before a normal service could be resumed.

About two weeks were to elapse before the shop was anything like dry and there was considerable damage done to stock on the counters and to bulk drugs in the cellars. Repairs, which were put in hand immediately, cost £88.

Boots, like a number of other shops ran a library service whereby one could borrow books, generally novels, for 1d per week. These commercial ventures supplemented the public libraries but like many other fine old practices had died a lingering death by the early sixties.

At the St Peter Port branch, the Head Librarian was Miss Marion Key. This department became yet another of the local success stories. Having seen the Gestapo take away a fair number of books which were considered to be offensive to the Third Reich, Miss Kay sweetly drew the attention of the German policeman to a book by a Dr. Goebbels. "Do not worry, that one is quite all right" came the grave response.

Realising that with a static stock of books, sooner or later every subscriber would have read every book in the library, Boots, very early on in the Occupation, started buying-in the personal libraries of customers. These transactions were done with great tact and understanding but had the twin advantages of realising cash for the needy customer and enlarging the stock of books available to subscribers.

In March 1940, i.e. prior to the invasion, there were 877 subscribers and the monthly takings were £19. This dropped to £15 in August 1940 but by March 1944 there were 1,981 subscribers. This figure disguises the fact that when the British-born islanders were deported, the library lost a large number of faithful subscribers in one go. Once again, Boots provided a morale boosting service. With the local cinemas showing mainly German propaganda films, the islanders tended to give their night-out at the cinema a miss. With varying types of curfews in place, what more natural than to curl up with a good book and forget the outside world for a while? Of course, with little or no electric light, most books were read by candlelight. Who supplied the books? Why Boots of course!

CHAPTER EIGHT

DELIVERANCE DEFERRED

Early on 6th June 1944 the residents of Guernsey were woken-up by the sound of gunfire and of hundreds of aircraft flying overhead. Although some distance away, it was clear that a major operation was taking place beyond Cherbourg, which was, of course, the D-Day landings. The residents of Guernsey must surely have felt that liberation was on hand although few would have thought through the method by which it would have been achieved. There was no strategic objective in trying to take Guernsey by force of arms. Unfortunately, logic flew out of the window when Vice Admiral Friedrich Huffmeier took over-all command for here was a dyed-in-the-wool Nazi who made Adolf Hitler seem almost reasonable!

Indeed, such was the fanatical determination of Huffmeier to defend Guernsey to the last man, that he would only address his own troops if they had been disarmed first! None of these strategic considerations were of much comfort to the islanders who saw their state of occupation gradually slip into a state of siege. After the initial jubilation, the islanders reconciled themselves to further months under the Nazi yoke.

Conditions gradually worsened on Guernsey and by late November 1944, the supply of electricity to the premises of Boots ceased entirely. Private houses still had current for about four hours in the evenings. Lack of power meant that the electric lift was inoperable and all heavy barrels, sacks and other merchandise had to be handled up and down the narrow stairs by the staff. The shop was designed to be lit artificially, for even on the very sunniest days, little light came into the building especially in the drug and toilet counters and the library. Arthur Butterworth instructed that certain counters were to be moved into the most advantageous sites and on the busiest days candles and night lights were used to illuminate the shop. However, the supply of these soon dried up. Conditions were particularly difficult on the drug and toilet counters making it impossible for staff to see what denomination of note was being offered. Indeed, staff had to take the notes for examination to the dispensary which was reasonably well lit from natural sources. The staff made little of this extra irritant and carried on in a spirit of good humour.

A more serious side effect of the loss of electric power was that powders and ointments could no longer be mixed except by hand. On 27th November 1944, the bread ration was reduced from 4.5 lbs to 3lbs per head per week. The former ration was almost inadequate, the new level totally so. Should the reader have in mind an issue of freshly baked golden brown loaves let such thoughts be discounted. The bread was made with one quarter part of cattle oats, which had been in stock for some time and had become mouldy and the result was a loaf that was quite unpalatable. The potato ration of 5lbs per head per week was maintained. Root vegetables were in very short supply and cabbages and other greens virtually unobtainable unless one had time to queue in the market for several hours. Rumours started that the International Red Cross were to send a relief ship.

In the true spirit of the Boots staff, Arthur Butterworth kept the administration of the branch up to date. He paid the income tax bill which had been outstanding since 1940 and reached agreement with the Inspector to leave further payments in abeyance until after the war. Tax Inspectors are a peculiar breed the whole world over and war or no war, having got his money for 1940, the Guernsey Inspector then asked for a full return of profits for the years 1941 to 1944. Arthur Butterworth parried with the statement that he would comply providing the Inspector took the return as provisional. Satisfied, Mr

Butterworth then instructed a firm of auditors to make up a profit and loss account covering the missing years.

November slipped into December and the long awaited Red Cross relief ship, the SS Vega arrived from Lisbon. One parcel was distributed to every member of the population with one more held in reserve. Although the Germans were scrupulous in not appropriating any of the consignment for their own use, they tried reducing the existing scale of rations on the grounds that the general population had received a nourishing food parcel and were thus not dependent upon the normal civilian ration. The monthly ration of meat, 4 ounces, was first increased to 8 ounces for the Christmas week-end but was then reduced to 3 ounces. Christmas week duly arrived and Arthur Butterworth sent each member of staff the following letter.

"I should like to take this opportunity of thanking you all for your loyal support during 1944 and for your cheerful acceptance of the increasingly trying conditions. I know that the curtailment of electric light and gas and the meagre rations which we are getting today together with the many annoying inconveniences and restrictions, are not consistent with the best work, but you have shewn that it is possible to give good service even under these conditions.

On behalf of the Firm, I am paying an extra fortnight's salary to all members of the regular staff and any members of the temporary staff who were with us in 1940. All other members of staff who have been with us for three months or more, will be paid an extra week's salary. With very best wishes to all of you for a much more cheerful and victorious New Year."

Yours sincerely

A. F. Butterworth

A list of the recipients of this bonus payment is shown in Appendix 4.

January 1945 came in with a vengeance. The month was extremely cold with strong biting north-easterly winds and the average temperature in the shop was 40 degrees Fahrenheit. The flooding of the previous August (as a result of the misplaced British shell) made the shop very damp and clammy. The bread ration was still 3lbs per head per week but the butter ration was reduced to two ounces per week and then discontinued after the "Vega" parcels were distributed.

It was impossible to make most of the manufactured lines, such as carrageen emulsion, laxative emulsions etc., without heat and Mr. Butterworth gave instructions for the old fireplace to be unbricked and put into use again. Boots were given a small ration of wood by the States of Guernsey but this was inadequate so it became necessary to tear up floor boards from one of the disused attics to supplement the official ration. There was a marked deterioration in the health of all staff and there was much absenteeism through sickness.

The shop then suffered a burglary, entry being effected via the trap-door from the air raid shelter which was previously thought to be burglar-proof. The shop lost 54 pounds of babies' rusks, 50 pounds of baby food and 280 packets of saccharin tablets kept for diabetics. Trade on the island was practically at a standstill with the grocers, who until then had managed to keep their full staff in employment, forced to give notice to all but the oldest employees as there was no work for them.

Rations were by then negligible and for one week in January all the grocers had to distribute was 2 ounces of macaroni per head and people were looking haggard. There was no fuel, boxwood which once sold for 6d (2.5p) a bundle went up in price to 4/3d (21p) and there were very long queues to get it. Undoubtedly, without the Red Cross parcels, the situation would have been extremely dire.

Things took a slight up-turn in February as the SS Vega turned up again with two parcels for each member of the population and 190 cases of drugs and chemists' sundries which were shared amongst all of the island's chemists. Arthur Butterworth reported that it was good to see the old familiar "Boots" cases and preparations and noted that in spite of five years of wartime conditions, Boots in England were managing to turn out goods very much of a pre-war quality which compared very favourably with the shoddy temporary war-time packs of French and German patent products. Many of the cases contained invalid and infant foods and it was very hard for the half-starved porters to appear unconcerned, as they unpacked items such as chocolate Ryvita which was destined for the hospitals.

On 13th February, there was no bread ration available. This was the worst blow yet suffered and everyone was hoping for flour to be sent on the SS Vega. People took this last blow bravely, but the younger members of the staff were getting more and more listless as a result of their short and ill-balanced rations. Rations for the week ended 17th February consisted of 5lbs of potatoes, 2lbs of root vegetables, 2 pints of skimmed milk, no greens, no bread, no meat and no butter or other fats.

The German troops were now beginning to look very un-military and quite a few were obviously sick. Many cats and dogs were disappearing and any pet rabbits not taken indoors at night were unlikely to be around to see the next sunrise. On 25th February, all electricity ceased and people tended to retire to bed as soon as darkness fell. A fortunate few still had candles but those who relied upon oil lamps had no paraffin available.

Matters deteriorated further in March 1945. Root vegetables and potatoes became unavailable. Skimmed milk was available only once in every five days, however some bread was put on sale. Water had been cut-off for sewerage purposes and German engineers had been going around from house to house sealing off all water outlets except for one tap for drinking. In April, a long held suspicion that some members of the shop staff had been engaged in petty pilfering came to a head. This was understandable although not excusable. A member of the drug department had been suspended for theft of tartaric acid and bicarbonate of soda and Arthur Butterworth was compelled to warn all staff of the seriousness of theft, even in the extreme circumstances under which they all worked and lived.

On the evening of 4th April 1945, Mr. Butterworth was called out by the Police who found one of the shop front doors ajar. Upon inspecting the premises, he found one of the boiler house windows was not properly closed and an iron bar wrenched out of the wall. It was obvious that this was an "inside job" doctored to look like a break-in. After police investigation, it was found that W. Ayres, the second porter, had hidden an accomplice in the lift shaft after letting him in during working hours. After the staff had gone for the night, the accomplice, a Mr. Dunning, let his father into the premises and together they took away 25 lbs of baby rusks and 12 lbs of baby food, some of which was subsequently recovered. The offenders were duly charged and sentenced, Ayres and Dunning (junior) getting six months hard labour and Dunning (senior) four months.

The position of porter was quite a commonplace employment in those days, since there were no delivery vans or bicycles. One enterprising chap, whether from Boots or somewhere else is not known, used to wander around St Peter Port with a sack on his shoulders in which was secreted a camera. One of his photographic efforts follows and shows a military train about to turn on to White Rock Pier. Given the circumstances of this "snap" it reflects very highly on the skill of the photographer. As to what the end result was, is open to question. Had he been discovered he would have been shot on sight. Even if he had uncovered something of inestimable value to the Allies, quite how he would have transmitted it to London is hard to envisage however, top marks for effort.

May brought liberation, in the nick of time. On Tuesday 8th May 1945, the war in Europe was at an end. Admiral Huffmeier, however, still needed to be convinced. A meeting took place on HMS Bulldog between English and German officers but all that Admiral Huffmeier was prepared to offer was an armistice and a warning that as the official German surrender did not come into effect until one minute past midnight, HMS Bulldog had better retreat pretty swiftly if they did not wish to be fired upon. After some fairly terse signals between the Captain of HMS Bulldog and Admiral Huffmeier a second rendezvous was organised and at 0714 on 9th May the official

Clandestine picture of German Military Train

surrender of Guernsey garrison was signed on the quarter-deck of HMS Bulldog. There is perhaps some sweet irony in that it was the Bulldog which captured an Enigma machine from a German U-Boat in 1941, an event which made a considerable impact on the work done at Bletchley and helped immeasurably in winning the war.

HM ships Bulldog and Beagle then moved to the south of St Peter Port and it was all over bar the shouting. The shouting, of which there was much, has been very competently described in the many books which covered the Occupation in a wider sense and it is not the object of this book to deal with that aspect.

Arthur Butterworth, like the true "company man" he was had already prepared his letter to his regional office on 7th May ready to catch the first post. Another man might have allowed himself a congratulatory pat on the back, but not Arthur.

Boots the Chemists
High Street
Guernsey
7th May 1945

Mr. R. L. Scorgie
Area Director
Boots the Chemists
Wimborne

Dear Mr. Scorgie,
　　Things are beginning to happen with great rapidity and it looks as though we shall be in touch with you in the very near future. I am getting this letter ready so that I can post it at the earliest opportunity.
　　Since October, I have been making monthly reports and during the month of October, I made up a report giving some details of how we fared since 1st July 1940. It is very difficult to believe that things are about to change, we have become so used to the same humdrum existence. Boredom has been our chief enemy here. We have had no tobacco for the last few months and this has been one of the worst factors from my own personal point of view.
　　You will be glad to know that the staff, few of whom you will know, are pretty well and in the best of spirits. They will need some holding when the great day comes. We are anxiously waiting to get news from England. We know that you must have had a terrible time in the south and only hope that our staffs have not suffered too much.
　　With regard to re-stocking this branch, I imagine you will have made arrangements for an opening order. If it is possible at this stage to manage priority for some classes of goods, I badly need drugs and packed goods, proprietories can wait. I expect that I shall have to share the first batch of goods with local chemists until they can make arrangements with their suppliers. Other goods which we badly need are razor blades, tooth and nail brushes and of course, toilet and household soaps.
　　I shall also need the help of at least one qualified man. I shall be very busy indeed getting ready for normal business and also winding-up the supplies of Red Cross drugs for the States, and it would be very helpful to have a man here who is conversant with things on the other side. (Some of us will probably need a little re-educating in routine work after five years separation.)

Yours sincerely

A. F. Butterworth

CHAPTER NINE

A TEAM EFFORT

Arthur Butterworth was very much aware that loyalty worked in both directions. Thus as well as expecting his staff to work for him, as manager he was aware that at the same time, their success was his success. He made this very clear in his report to his head office from which the following are but a few examples. There was only one rotten apple in a barrel of some thirty-six employees, which speaks volumes for Mr. Butterworth's skill as a manager.

Mr. H. Ord

Worked on the drug counter during the entire period, doing much the same work as in peace time. Had very little time off as he could not be spared. Learnt the art of making and fitting trusses and helped Nurse in this respect.

Mr. F. Dickson

Put in charge of the Drug Manufacturing Department at the outset and put his very best into the job. He overcame the many difficulties which faced him in a loyal and painstaking way.

Mrs. Rich (née Miss M. Coombe)

In charge of the toiletry department which she ran before the war. Has done good work with window and counter displays, work which would have earned her great credit in peace-time.

Nurse A. Giles

Her duties were very different from those in pre-occupation days and she has used her ingenuity in making everything which could be made for the benefit of the customers. She manufactured such things as corn plasters, suspensory and calico bandages, trusses, both spring and web, she made sanitary towels and finger stalls at home with the help of her mother and everything she did was to the highest standards.

Miss R. Le Pelley

Worked hard, always against the odds. It was impossible to augment her department from abroad but she took endless trouble to augment her stocks with bags, etc., made by herself, mostly in her own time. These were of surprisingly good standard and eagerly sought by customers.

Miss P. Robinson

I knew she would make a splendid assistant when she joined us in 1941 but she proved to be far better than my expectations. She is most reliable, has balance, initiative, a dignified manner and a business brain. She is very hard-working and puts in much extra time on her own initiative. Customers are continually remarking to me how they like to be served by Miss Robinson. She has been of inestimable value to me and I really do not know how we would have got on without her.

Mr. H. de la Mothe

His chief anxiety was that when the evacuation was underway, if he left he would have no work to do. I assured him that I would guarantee him work of some kind, so he decided to stay with me. In the event it was fortunate that he stayed because there was plenty of picture framing to do after people had settled down and realised that we could still execute such work. When we exhausted our stock of moulding, wood was bought locally, as were old picture frames.

Everything sent out was up to pre-war standard, and over three thousand framing orders were executed. I have nothing but praise for his work. He has given untiring devotion to his job and never allowed himself to have a slack moment.

Mrs. Dorey

Mrs Dorey was the charlady and was about 67 when the war started. She has been with the firm for many years and although she could have earned £3 per week working for the Germans in an easier job, she refused to leave us. She has much extra work to do including the shop's washing which was no minor matter since it included all of the manufacturing side's washing. She had little soap or fuel and I have recently found out that for a long time, she has, at the age of 71 years, been collecting fuel at nights from the woods and hedgerows to use in the shop. She has been very cheerful all along and refused to let things get her down.

CHAPTER TEN

THE CAPTAINS AND THE KINGS DEPART

Life swiftly returned to normal in Guernsey. The occupying troops were first set to work in mine clearance, etc., then sent to POW camps on mainland Britain. One of the more startling consequences was that shortly after the end of the Occupation, Arthur Butterworth sent to his head office a cheque for £51,613/12/10d representing the retained profits earned during the war years. This is approximately equivalent to £1,300,000 in today's money! Boots rewarded Mr. Butterworth with a small monetary sum and promotion to the Board of Boots (Cash Chemists) Western Ltd. Since he carried on working in Guernsey until he retired in 1959, this must have been a bit of an "Irishman's promotion". Matthew Angell also received a small monetary reward, the exact amount he has now forgotten but described by him as being "very acceptable". Upon the retirement of Arthur Butterworth, Matthew took over as Manager until he, in turn, retired in June 1973. After Arthur Butterworth retired, he remained in Guernsey until his death. It is believed that he hailed from Gloucestershire. He and Matthew first met at the Commercial Road (Portsmouth) branch of Boots when Matthew was a student in that city.

To mark Matthew's retirement, the staff of the Guernsey branch of Boots presented him with an aluminium-framed greenhouse and a scroll signed by over one hundred past and present friends. The Territorial Pharmacists Association presented him with a camera and a dinner at the Old Government House Hotel for Matthew and his wife was attended by some seventy-six persons. As well as being a true and faithful servant of Boots, Matthew found time to serve as a douzenier (councillor) for the parish of St Andrews for some twenty years and also served as President and Secretary of the Guernsey branch of the Pharmaceutical Society.

In July 1986, in recognition of his name being on the register of the Pharmaceutical Society for fifty years, the local branch honoured Matthew with a formal dinner and the presentation of a teak garden chair as well as installing him as Honorary Chairman. The certificate reads:

10th October 1986
This is to certify that
Matthew Nicholas Angel MPS
has been appointed Honorary Chairman
of The Guernsey Branch of the
Pharmaceutical Society of Great Britain.
The election to this office marks his 50 years as a Pharmacist
and also recognises his outstanding contribution to the practice of
pharmacy in Guernsey

The author has had the great privilege of talking to and corresponding with Matthew, now a sprightly eighty-seven year old and still as sharp as ever. When submitting various drafts of this book for his approval, no detail, however small, escaped his attention. It is only fitting therefore to let Matthew Angell MPS have the last word.

"Britain was at war, and we were British.
Times were grim - we had many problems and
we overcame most of them.
Looking back on it now I would not have
missed the experience for anything."

EPILOGUE

"What we owe to the
pharmacists for their work
during the Occupation
only the medical profession knows.
They should have had more public
recognition than, in fact, they ever did."

Dr. Douglas J. Gow
President of the Jersey branch
of the Pharmaceutical Society

Appendix 1

A small selection of items manufactured by, or under the supervision of Matthew Angell, Pharmacist, Boots the Chemists, St Peter Port, Guernsey

Stearic acid	Iodine
Lozenges	Permanganate of potash solution
Pastilles	Tinctures of chloroform and morphine
Quinine suppositories	Veterinary embrocation
Lactic acid suppositories	Gargles
Glycerine suppositories	Mist. (mixture) ammonia chloride concentrate
Baby and Invalid rusks	Mist camphor compound
Yeast granules	Mist expectorant concentrate
Baby food	Ung (ointment) cremor antisepticus
Styptic and Caustic pencils	Suppositories of cocaine and morphine
Menthol inhalers	Tinctures of Belladonna
Syrup of codeine	Tinctures of Capsicum
Veganin substitute	Magnesium sulphate paste
Laxatives	Tinctures of Digitalis
Gees' Linctus	Unguent of sulphur
Calamine lotion	Liquid of Arsenicalis
Gentian violet	Digitalis pills

Appendix 2

List of goods made by the Toiletry Manufacturing Department of Boots the Chemists 1940 to 1944

Hair cream, (oily and non-oily)
Wave setting lotion
Brilliantine
Magnesia toothpaste
Magnesia tooth powder
Carbolic tooth powder
Regadent
Baby powder
Talcum powder
Skin food
Vanishing and cleansing cream
Skin tonic
Shaving cream
After shave lotion
Face powder

Powder puffs
Washing squares and gloves
Sark lavender sachets
Hand cream
Foot powder
Bath crystals and salts
Hair tonic and shampoo
Bay rum
Deodor
Perfumes
Calamine and sunburn lotion
Hair and face powder
Adhesive paste for own use
Cutical remover
Theatrical greasepaints

Appendix 3

An experiment to determine the Vitamin A content of oils extracted from sundry fish livers.

Eleven healthy adult guinea pigs of average weight, 29 ounces, were fed on a diet deficient in Vitamin A, the diet consisting of beetroot and oats, or boiled potatoes and oats. At the end of five weeks, one animal was found to be passing blood and to be suffering from diarrhoea. At the end of the sixth week, this animal died and upon examination it was noticed that the intestinal wall was very thin and that fermentation had been going on inside the intestine. At the end of eleven weeks, the average weight had dropped to 26 ounces, several of the animals were in poor condition and some were passing blood.

At the end of week twelve, all ten guinea pigs were suffering from a disease of the eyelids and all except three, appeared very sick. They were then given daily doses of fish liver oil. By now however, the guinea pigs were so ill that five died in the next three weeks through intestinal trouble. However, two days after the commencement of the doses of fish oil, there was a great improvement in the eyelids and on the third day, all eyelids were noticeably better.

At the start of week fourteen the average weight had dropped but during this week, there was a reversal of this weight loss. The supply of fish oil was ceased but as weight levels dropped again, was recommenced the following week. Three of the remaining animals were now quite healthy but two were still unwell. These two were placed in separate hutches one being fed on a normal diet and the other on normal diet supplemented with fish oil. The one on a normal diet died but the one whose diet was supplemented with fish oil gradually increased in weight until quite recovered and is now a normal healthy guinea pig.

As is already well-known, animals which are deprived of Vitamin A develop a disease of the eyelids but in this particular instance, this was reversed by the administration of the fish oil. From these experiments it can be deduced that the locally produced fish oil has an ample Vitamin A content so as to be a reasonable substitute for Cod Liver oil.

M. N. Angell MPS

Author's note:
The above report has been slightly condensed from the original.

Appendix 4

BONUS PAYMENTS MADE
CHRISTMAS 1944

NAME	BONUS	POSITION
Mr. F. Dickson	£9.14.10d	Drug Manufacturing
Miss P. Robinson	£3.16.11d	Drug Department
Mr. E. Worth	£3.10. 6d	Dispensers Assistant
Mr. E. Doutch	£2.19.10d	Drug Department
Miss Le Tissier	£1. 9.11d	Apprentice, drug department
Nurse A. Giles	£8.10.11d	Surgical Department
Miss M. Gillson	£1.18. 6d	Surgical Department
Mrs. Rich	£5.16. 5d	Toiletries
Miss Tostevin	£2.15. 7d	Toiletries
Miss H. Gallienne	£1. 1. 4d	Toiletries
Miss Kilby	£1. 0. 3d	Toiletries
Miss A. Rose	£3.18. 0d	Cashier
Miss Syvet	£1. 0. 3d	Library
Miss R. Le Pelley	£4. 3. 4d	No. 2 Department
Miss B. O' Meara	£3. 6. 3d	No. 2 Department
Miss M. Key	£5. 9. 0d	Library
Mrs. Collas	£4. 4. 5d	Library
Miss M. Toy	£2.10. 2d	Drug Manufacturing
Miss Udle	£2.10. 2d	Drug Manufacturing
Miss B. Gallienne	£1. 0. 3d	Drug Manufacturing
Miss J. Palzeard	13.11d	Drug Manufacturing
Miss Osborne	19. 3d	Drug Manufacturing
Miss Gilman	£1. 2. 5d	Toiletry Manufacturing
Miss Gorelle	£1. 3. 6d	Toiletry Manufacturing
Mr. H. Patch	£5.19. 8d	Porter
Mr. W. Ayres	£4. 2. 3d	Porter
Mr. de la Mothe	£6.19.11d	Picture Framer
Mr. E. Cochrane	£1.12.10d	Bottle Washer
Mr. T. Keyho	£1. 0. 3d	Messenger
Mrs. Dorey	£2. 9. 2d	Charwoman
Miss Williams	£1. 3. 6d	Bottle Woman
Mrs. Hammond	£13. 6d	Charwoman